The Simple Answer to Using **Excel 97**

This guide has been produced by Sue Rowley and Chris Vaughan, who used to lecture at Wakefield College with special responsibility for resource-based learning in information technology.

© Information Technology Resources 1999

For further copies, please contact us: Phone: 01977 679221   Fax: 01977 673352
                                         E-mail: help@it-resources.co.uk
                                         www.it-resources.co.uk

Published by: Information Technology Resources (ITR), Bridgefoot House, Marsh Lane, Beal, East Yorkshire, DN14 0SL.

Printed by: York Publishing Services, 64 Hallfield Road, Layerthorpe, York, YO3 7XQ.

ISBN 0 9534860 3 6

INDEX

INDEX

Information Technology Resources – User Guide for EXCEL 99
© ITR 11021

INDEX

INDEX

Information Technology Resources – User Guide for EXCEL 99
© ITR 11021

INDEX

INDEX

Information Technology Resources – User Guide for EXCEL 99
© ITR 11021

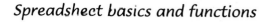

INDEX

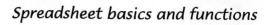

INDEX

Information Technology Resources – User Guide for EXCEL 99
© ITR 11021

Welcome to The Simple Answer To Using Excel 97

This is a very valuable resource if you are:

- a new user to Excel;
- using Excel at home;
- using Excel at work;
- following a programme of study at school, college or university;
- converting from another spreadsheet application;
- an extensive user, and you have taught yourself; or
- an infrequent user.

This simple, easy-to-follow reference guide will support your spreadsheet needs at home, in the workplace, throughout your programme of study and during the examination and assessment process.

The Simple Answer to using Excel 97

This guide aims to:

- help **you** use Excel 97 through a simple, relevant, practical guided approach;
- increase your confidence and productivity when using Excel 97;
- help you to use the software correctly and efficiently;
- provide information and support as and when **you** need it;
- provide a simple, quick, reference guide on how to use the different features and techniques of Excel 97;
- support specific techniques and skills needed for IT Key Skills; and
- support the spreadsheet part of CLAIT, IBT II and III training, examination and assessment.

How do I ...?

<u>Use this guide</u>

We introduce the features of Excel 97 through the question How do I ...? followed by a simple, concise guide on how to carry out the function.

In this guide we present the range of options available to carry out a specific function. We present options in the following order: 'icon or button' 🖨 , keyboard shortcut keys, for example, **'Ctrl P'** (**hold down** the Control key [see page 5] and **press 'P'**); or 'pull down' menu. Instructions such as **'File', 'Print'** mean **pull down** the **'File'** menu and **click** on the **'Print'** option.

Bold text means you should take action, in other words press a button on the computer or observation, for example, using a dialogue box.

A down arrow at the side of a box shows there are further options. **Click** on this to reveal the list.

<u>Quick reference section</u>

We have included information on getting started, keyboard layout, using the mouse, windows, menus, toolbars, scrolling, settings, help, keyboard shortcuts and much, much more that you will find useful as an introduction. We also include information on workbooks and worksheets, how to create formulae, operators used in formulae and troubleshooting.

Throughout the guide, we have included pictures of the screen to give you an idea of what will happen on screen.

The keyboard

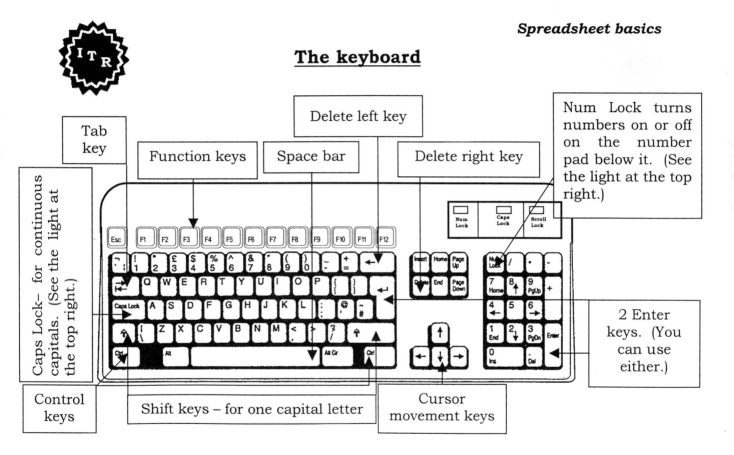

Delete left key

Tab key

Function keys

Space bar

Delete right key

Num Lock turns numbers on or off on the number pad below it. (See the light at the top right.)

Caps Lock– for continuous capitals. (See the light at the top right.)

2 Enter keys. (You can use either.)

Control keys

Shift keys – for one capital letter

Cursor movement keys

The mouse

The mouse is a pointing device. Move the mouse in any direction and the pointer moves on screen. You will use the left mouse button in most circumstances. There are 4 functions.

- **Pointing** – placing the mouse pointer over an item.
- **Clicking** – pressing and releasing the left button.
- **Double clicking** – tapping the left button twice rapidly and releasing.
- **Dragging** – clicking and holding down the left button while moving the mouse pointer.

If you are left-handed, you can reset the mouse to use the right button. **Click** on the **'Start'** button, **'Settings'**, **'Control Panel'**, **'Mouse'** and **'Left-handed'**.

Access Excel

The Windows operating system will load to the desktop (opening screen).

Double click the left mouse button on the Microsoft Excel icon (picture) (if one is available).

Or, you can **click** on the **'Start'** button on the 'taskbar', and **click** on **'Programs'** and **'Microsoft Excel'**.

Excel has certain settings which always apply unless you change them. These include screen settings, fonts (see page 63), the toolbars (see page 19), number of sheets for each workbook (see page 20) and so on.

Disadvantages of a paper-based system

A budget usually uses columns and rows of text and numbers, as shown below. You have to work out the figures in the 'Balance' column.

Household budget for January

	Spending	Income	Balance
Mortgage	£350	£1020	£670
Council Tax	£55		£615
Electricity	£43		£572

The disadvantages of a paper-based document (which includes calculations) are given below.

- It takes longer if you have to work out calculations yourself.
- You can make mistakes when transferring numbers.
- If you make a mistake in a number, it can change other calculations.
- If an item of spending changes, you will have to rub out the wrong numbers and work out new totals.

<u>What is a spreadsheet in Excel</u>

Excel creates electronic spreadsheets which you can use to input, analyse and manage data involving numbers, for example budgets or forecasts. You will do calculations using formulae, which update automatically when you change any related entries.

A spreadsheet is a grid of 'cells' organised into columns and rows. Columns are identified by letters, and rows by numbers. Where the columns and rows meet is called a 'cell'. This has a 'cell reference' made up of the column letter and row number, for example 'C3' is column C and row 3.

	A	B	C	D	E	F	G	H
1								
2								
3								
4								
5								

The cell which has a bold border round it is the 'active cell'. When you key-in text or numbers these appear in the 'active cell'.

Advantages of using an electronic spreadsheet

	A	B	C	D
1	Household budget for January			
2				
3		Spending	Income	Balance
4	Mortgage	£350	£1,020	£670
5	Council Tax	£55		£615
6	Electricity	£43		£572

	A	B	C	D
1	Household budget for January			
2				
3		Spending	Income	Balance
4	Mortgage	350	1020	=C4-B4
5	Council Tax	55		=D4-B5+C5
6	Electricity	43		=D5-B6+C6

In the above example, we have transferred the paper-based document shown on page 8 to an electronic spreadsheet. On the left it shows figures in the balance column. On the right it shows the formulae we used to work out these figures.

- Any changes to the figures in the spending or income column, will automatically change the balance.
- You can copy formulae so that you do not have to carry out the same calculation several times.
- You can check the formulae to see the answers are correct without doing any further working out.
- Changing text or numbers is very easy.

Workbooks and worksheets

Excel stores its data in a 'workbook'. A 'workbook' is a file and is automatically named 'Book' followed by a number, unless you save it with a different name (see page 54). Each 'workbook' always contains 3 'worksheets' but you can add others up to 255. 'Worksheets' can contain more than one page and are useful for organising related data into topic areas. You will see the 'worksheets' at the bottom of the screen and they are named 'Sheet 1', 'Sheet 2' and 'Sheet 3'. You can easily change these names to identify their contents (see page 96).

'Sheet 1' automatically appears on screen when you open the 'workbook' and the 'active sheet' is displayed with a white background. To open another sheet, **click** with the left mouse button on the sheet name.

Data (information) can be either 'text', 'numbers', 'dates', 'times', 'formulae' (see page 45) or 'functions' (see page 48).

Key to opening screen of Excel

1 Title bar including document name
2 Menu bar
3 Standard toolbar
4 'Select All' button
5 Active cell
6 Name box (cell reference area)
7 Formula bar
8 Formatting toolbar
9 Minimize, Restore and Close buttons for Excel
10 Minimize, Restore and Close buttons for the workbook
11 Column titles
12 Row titles
13 Sheet tabs
14 Status bar
15 Taskbar
16 Scroll bars
17 End of page marker

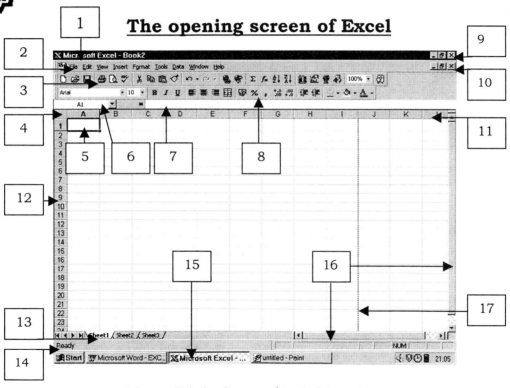

The opening screen of Excel

Labels: 1, 2, 3, 4, 5, 6, 7, 8, 9, 10, 11, 12, 13, 14, 15, 16, 17

<u>Mouse pointers in spreadsheets</u>

The mouse pointer changes depending upon where you place it on the screen.

This is the normal pointer shown when you place the mouse over the worksheet area, used for 'selecting' cells (see pages 23 and 24).

+ This symbol appears when you point the mouse at the 'fill handle', (see page 68) – the small square at the bottom right-hand corner of the bordered 'active cell' (see pages 9 and 11). You can 'drag' this up, down, left or right and use it for copying formulae and data.

This is displayed when you 'point' the mouse at the border of the 'active cell' and you use it to 'drag and drop' (move) and with the 'Ctrl' key to copy data. It also appears when you 'point' the mouse at the 'menu bar' or the 'toolbars'.

I This is the 'I-beam' and appears in the 'formula bar' (see pages 12 and 13) and 'active cell'. It appears when you are editing or entering data.

Keyboard shortcuts

You can use the keyboard rather than 'menus' or 'toolbars'. **Hold down** the 'Control' key and 'Shift' key, if shown, and **press** the next key.

Bold	Ctrl B or Ctrl 2	New document	Ctrl N
Cancel entry in active cell	Esc	New line within a cell	Alt Enter
Close	Ctrl W or Ctrl F4	Open a document	Ctrl O
Copy	Ctrl C	Paste	Ctrl V
Create a chart	F11	Paste name into a formula	F3
Currency format	Ctrl Shift $	Print	Ctrl P
Cut	Ctrl X	Repeat formatting	F4
Edit contents of cells	F2	Replace	Ctrl H
Exit Excel	Alt F4	Save a document	Ctrl S
Find	Ctrl F	Save As	F12
Format cells	Ctrl 1	Show formulae	Ctrl
Go to	Ctrl G or F5	Spellcheck	F7
Insert a new worksheet	Shift F11	Strikethrough	Ctrl 5
Italics	Ctrl I or Ctrl 3	Standard toolbar on/off	Ctrl 7
Move to next pane	F6	Underline	Ctrl U or Ctrl 4
Move to next workbook	Ctrl tab or Ctrl F6	Undo	Ctrl Z

Move around the screen using the keyboard

You can move the cursor with the cursor movement keys (see page 5), the mouse or the keyboard. Some quick cursor movements are shown below.

Cell to the right	'Tab' or →
Cell to the left	←
Up one row	↑
Down one row	↓
Beginning of row (column A)	'Home'
End of row or to next blank cell	'Ctrl' →
Beginning of column or to next blank cell	'Ctrl' ↑
End of column or to next blank cell	'Ctrl' ↓
Beginning of worksheet	'Ctrl' 'Home'
End of worksheet (last entry)	'Ctrl' 'End'
Up one screen	'Page Up'
Down one screen	'Page Down'
Next worksheet	'Ctrl' 'Page Down'
Previous worksheet	'Ctrl' 'Page Up'
Keep selected cells highlighted and move round sheet	'Scroll Lock', **select** cells, arrow keys

Minimize, maximize and move windows

At the top right of the screen there are 2 sets of 3 buttons ▬⊡✕ for changing the size of the window.

The top set of buttons applies to Excel, the bottom set is for the current workbook.

Click on the top 'Minimize' ▬ button and Excel is shrunk on to the 'taskbar' at the bottom of the screen. The 'taskbar' displays the Excel logo and start of the file name. **Click** on the logo to 'Maximize' the screen.

Click on the top 'Restore' ⊡ button to change from full screen to 2 windows. **Click** on the 'Maximize' ☐ button to show the full screen again.

To move a window, **click** on the 'title bar' (see pages 12 and 13) and **drag** the window to a new position.

Click on the bottom 'Close' ✕ button to exit (leave) the workbook and the top 'Close' button to exit Excel.

Pull-down menus

File	Edit	View	Insert	Format	Tools	Data	Window	Help

To use a menu, **point** to it and **click** the left mouse button. Or, **hold down** the **'Alt'** key and **press** the underlined letter in the menu title, for example, **'Alt f'** for the File menu. A list of options drops down. To select (choose) an option **point** and **click**. Inside the menus, certain items may be 'greyed-out', this means they are currently not available. Once a menu is open, move the mouse left or right to open other menus. To close a menu without making a choice, **click** anywhere outside it.

Inside menus, another way to select items is with the 'Alt' key and underlined letters. Some options have other keys, such as **'Ctrl o'** to open a 'workbook'. Dots after an option indicate a 'dialogue box' and ▶ shows there is another menu for you to look at.

↶ Undo Font	Ctrl+Z
↷ Repeat Font	Ctrl+Y
✂ Cut	Ctrl+X
🖹 Copy	Ctrl+C
📋 Paste	Ctrl+V
Paste Special...	
Paste as Hyperlink	
Fill	▶
Clear	▶
Delete...	
Delete Sheet	
Move or Copy Sheet...	
🔍 Find...	Ctrl+F
Replace...	Ctrl+H
Go To...	Ctrl+G
Links...	
Object	

<u>Toolbars</u>

The buttons carry out the same functions as the pull-down menus, but are faster and easier to use.

Point to each button and wait - the 'tooltip' is displayed which gives the function of the button. To select a function, **click** on the appropriate button. When buttons are 'greyed-out' they are currently not available for you to use.

To display further toolbars, **point** at an existing toolbar and **click** the right mouse button**.** Or, **click** on **'View', 'Toolbars'**. Then **click** on the toolbar you need with the left-hand button.

Change settings with 'Tools', 'Options'

You may want to change the 'default' settings for 'Excel' – those which always apply to every workbook, for example the number of worksheets you create for each workbook. This is set at '3'.

Click on **'Tools'**, **'Options'** to display a 'dialogue box'. **Click** on the 'General' tab to see this 'dialogue box'. In the 'Sheets in new workbook:' box, '3' is shown, **click** on the ▲ to increase this. Remember that any changes you make here will affect this and all future workbooks. Look through all the settings, but record any changes in case you want to return to the original settings in the future.

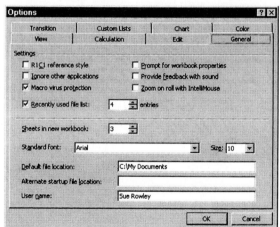

Change the size of your screen display

'Zoom' `100%` ▼ control is on the 'standard toolbar' and changes the size of the page on the screen. (The number may be different on your computer.)

The display is set at 100% so that the data is easy to read. **Click** on the down arrow to reveal the list of options and **select** another if this is not suitable.

Select a range of cells and **click** on 'Selection' to change the cells you have selected to the full size of the screen.

Resetting the 'Zoom control' does not change the size of letters in the final print out.

Scroll through a document

There are 2 ways of moving through a document to see the whole of the page, 'cursor movement keys' (see page 16) or the 'vertical and horizontal scroll bars'.

The 'vertical scroll bar' is at the right of the screen. **Click** on the up arrow to move towards the top of the page. **Click** on the down arrow to move towards the bottom of the page.

Click and **drag** the elevator (the grey lozenge) to move quickly through your document.

Click anywhere on the scroll bar above the lozenge to move up one screen and below the lozenge to move down one screen. The 'horizontal scroll bar' is at the bottom of the screen and works in the same way.

Select cells or a range of cells

Selecting (highlighting) cells by dragging over them with the mouse is a quick way of making your choice, but there are other ways. A range is several cells which are all next to each other.

Select a single cell	**Click** on the cell to make this the 'active cell'.
Select a range of cells	**'Shift'** ← → ↑ ↓.
Select from the 'active cell' to the top of the screen	**'Shift'** and **press 'Home'**.
Select a row	**Click** on the row title or **press 'Shift'** and **'spacebar'**.
Select a column	**Click** on the column title or **press 'Ctrl'** and **'spacebar'**.
Select worksheet	**Click** on **'Select All'** button (see pages 12 and 13) or **'Ctrl A'** or **'Ctrl' 'Shift'** and **'spacebar'**.
Select individual cells or ranges which are not next to each other	**'Ctrl', click** or **drag**.
Extend a selection around the 'active cell'	**Press 'F8'** and **click** on a cell. When you have done this **press 'F8'** to turn the function off.

Select cell contents for editing

You can select (highlight) text either on the 'formula bar' or in the 'active cell'. When a cell is 'active' its contents appear on the 'formula bar'. **Move** the mouse pointer over the data and the mouse pointer will change to an I-beam. **Click** to position the cursor. Or, you can **press F2** to place the cursor at the end of the data in the 'active cell'. Or, **double click** on the 'active cell' to move the cursor to within the cell.

Select a word	**Double click** on the word.
Select cell contents on 'formula bar'	**Position** your cursor at the beginning of the entry and **press 'Shift'** and **click**.
Select set text	**Click** at the beginning of your selection and **press 'Shift'** and **click** at the end.
Extend a selection	**'Shift'** and **click** at the new position.
Reduce a selection	**'Shift'** and **click** at the new position.
Select a character to the right	**'Shift'** →.
Select a character to the left	**'Shift'** ←.

The order in which you carry out calculations

You will use formulae to make calculations. The mathematical symbols used are as follows.

+   addition
-     subtraction
*   multiplication
/   division

You must make calculations in a precise order. For example, 5 + 3 * 6, would produce an answer of 23 not 48, as it would be if worked from left to right. Excel makes calculations in the order given below. As a result Excel would multiply 3 by 6 to make 18 and then add 5 to give the answer 23. Brackets are always calculated first so input (5 + 3) * 6 to produce the answer 48.

()   **B**rackets
/   **D**ivision
*   **M**ultiplication
+   **A**ddition
-      **S**ubtraction.   Remember this with **'BoDMAS'**.

Operators

%	Percent	=B3*15%
^	Exponentiation	=3^2 (This is the same as 3*3.)
=	Makes cells equal to each other	=C3
>	Greater than	=IF(A3>C3, "ORDER")
<	Lesser than	=IF(A3<C3, "")
>=	Greater than or equal to	=IF(A3>=C3, "ORDER")
<=	Lesser than or equal to	=IF(A3<=C3, "")
<>	Not equal to	=IF(B2<>H4, "NO BONUS"
:	Used to identify a range	=SUM(B3:B10)
,	Combines formulae and functions	=SUM(B3:B5,C3:C5)
&	Combines cell values into one entry	="Total "&SUM(B11:G11)
""	Identifies text in IF statements or, when placed together leaves cell empty	=IF(E7<100,"REORDER", "")
!	Identifies a reference as a sheet not a cell	=Sheet2!B1+Sheet1!E10

Get help

Click on **'Help'**, **'Contents and Index'** to display the Excel 'Help' with 3 different sections - 'Contents', 'Index' and 'Find'.

- Contents groups the help items into topics and this can be useful when you are first starting to use Excel.

- Index lists all the topics in alphabetical order. **Key-in** the first few letters of the function and it moves you to that area of the alphabet. **Double click** on the item you need.

- Find is the 'Help' database. **Key-in** the function and Excel searches for anything connected with that item. If the 'Minimize database size' option is recommended, **choose** it.

Press 'F1' or **Click** on [?] to open the 'Office Assistant'. **Key-in** your question and it will search for the answer. Use the **'Options'**, **'Gallery'** to change 'Clippit' (the Paperclip) to something else. Why not experiment with what you can do?

Troubleshooting

Formula error message will be shown if you use text in a cell where the formula needs numbers, or if you delete a cell used in the formula or if the cell is not wide enough to display the result of the formula.

Message	Reason	Action
#####	The column is not wide enough to display the result	Widen the column
#VALUE!	There is text in a number cell	Use a function which will ignore text
#DIV/0!	You are using a formula divided by 0 (zero)	Enter a number other than 0 or change the cell reference
#NAME?	Colon in a function formula has been left out	Check the formula
	Double quotes round text in a formula have been left out	Insert quotes as necessary
	The name of a function has been misspelt	Correct the spelling
	The name of a cell range has been misspelt	Correct the spelling
#REF!	There is a problem with a cell reference which has been deleted or moved	Check the formulae or restore the cell references
#NULL!	You are using an incorrect operator between ranges or cell references	Check there is a comma between the ranges or references

Files and folders

Effective file management will group together related files in folders (containers that can hold folders and files). You can view the folders and files stored on your computer in 'My Computer' or, you see the 'directory tree' in 'Windows Explorer'.

Click on **'Start'**, **'Programs'**, **'Windows Explorer'** to display the 'directory tree'. We identify folders by using the symbol ⬜. **Click** on a folder on the left of the window to open it and see the contents of the folder on the right. If a 'plus sign (+)' is shown there are further folders within that folder.

A 'file's icon' 📄 at the side of the workbook name, identifies its software. **Double click** on the 'icon' to open the software application (Excel) and the file. Documents will normally be saved in the 'My Documents' folder. To create a new folder inside 'My Documents', **click** to open it ⬜, **click** on **'File'**, **'New'**, **'Folder'** and **key-in** your name for the folder.

Move from one folder to another

When you open a file, the 'Open dialogue box' automatically looks in the 'My Documents' folder - the main storage area on the hard disk drive. If the folder you want to save your file in, is within the 'My Documents' folder, **double click** on the folder name to open it.

Think of the hard drive as shown below. Use the 'Up One Level' button to take you up through the different levels.

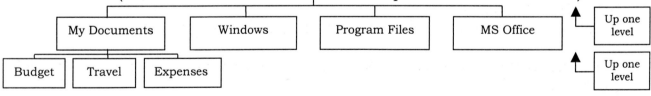

Spreadsheets' section

This section introduces the functions that you will use. We present the information in an easy-to-follow format, including how to:

- create worksheets;
- enter formulae;
- edit and format;
- improve the appearance of the spreadsheet;
- move and copy data;
- use IF statements;
- LOOKUP tables; and
- pivot tables to summarise and analyse data.

Keep the guide handy for quick reference on both new and previously-used functions.

Throughout the section, we have included pictures of the screen to give you an idea of what will happen on screen.

How do I ...?

<u>Create a spreadsheet</u>

Click on the 'New' button or **press** 'Ctrl n' to automatically begin a new workbook based on the 'Normal template'. A workbook is a file which contains 3 worksheets. However, you can add more (see pages 20 and 95). Each worksheet can contain many pages. You can use 'templates' (see page 107) for different styles, layouts and settings with your workbooks. 'Normal' is the one most people use.

Click on **'File', 'New'** to display this 'dialogue box'. (The 2 options mentioned above do not display this box). **Double click** on **'Workbook'** to load the 'Normal' template or choose **'Spreadsheet Solutions'** for other templates.

Remember when you key-in text it will appear in the 'active cell' (see page 9) when you press 'Enter'.

How do I ...?

Open an existing workbook or delete a workbook

Click on the 'Open' 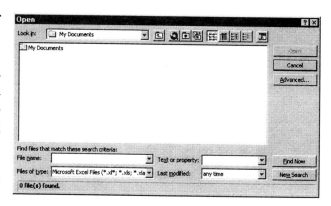 button or '**Ctrl o**' or '**File**', '**Open**' to display this 'dialogue box'.

Check the 'Look in:' box to make sure you are looking in the correct folder. Or, you can **click** on the 'Up One Level button' to find the folder you need (see pages 29 and 30).

Check 'Files of type:' – the box displays '**Microsoft Excel Files (*.xl*; *.xls; *.xla)**'.

When you have found the file, **double click** on the icon to the left of the filename, or **click** once and either **press** '**Enter**' or **click** on '**Open**'.

To delete an existing workbook, **click** on its file name and **press** '**Delete**'. The screen prompt will ask you to confirm that you want to delete.

How do I ...?

<u>Open another workbook and move between spreadsheets</u>

You can open several workbooks at once. At the 'Open' 'dialogue box' hold down the 'Ctrl' or the 'Shift' key to choose more than one file name. **Hold down** the 'Ctrl' key and **click** on individual files from different parts of the file list. You will use the 'Shift' key to select files that are grouped together. **Click** on the first file name, **hold down 'Shift'** and **click** on the last file name. **Click** on 'Open'.

To move between open workbooks **press 'Ctrl Tab'**, or **click** on **'Window'** on the 'menu bar'. At the bottom of the 'Window' menu is a list of all the open workbooks. The one you can see on screen has a tick at the side of it. To see another workbook, **click** on its name.

The 'Window' menu does not close down workbooks, it just allows you to move between open spreadsheets bringing a different one to the front for you to see. To close all open workbooks see page 59.

Information Technology Resources – User Guide for Excel 97
© ITR 1999

How do I ...?

Move around the worksheet using cell references

Each cell is identified by its reference, that is the letter of the column and number of the row which form the cell. To move to a cell, **click** on it with the left mouse button. When you do this its cell reference appears in the 'Name Box' on the 'formula bar' (see pages 12 and 13). However, if your spreadsheet is large, it is quicker to move by giving a cell reference.

Key-in the cell reference in the 'Name Box' and **press 'Enter'**. Or, **press 'F5'** or **'Ctrl G'** or **'Edit' 'Go To'** to display this 'dialogue box'. The cursor is in the 'Reference:' box. **Key-in** the cell reference and **click** on **'OK'**. Or, **double click** on the cell reference from the list shown.

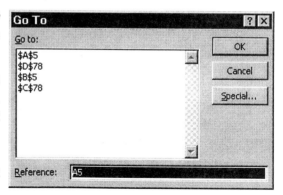

See page 16 for moving round the worksheet using the keyboard.

How do I ...?

Input numbers

The mouse pointer turns to a cross ⬧ when you place it over the worksheet. **Point** to the cell where the number is to appear and **click** to select it. This is now the 'active cell' (see page 9).

Key-in the number and it appears both in the cell and on the 'formula bar'. **Press 'Enter'** to enter the data into the cell. Or, **click** on the 'Enter' ✔ button on the 'formula bar', or **press 'Tab'** key or → or ↓. Numbers automatically line up at the right of the column. When you are keying-in numbers which are wider than the column, the column automatically adjusts to fit the number.

A1	▾	✕ ✔ =	568235.25
	A	B	C	D
1	568235.25			
2				

When you press 'Enter' or ↓ the 'active cell' moves to the cell below. When you click on the 'Enter' button, the 'active cell' will stay in the same place. The 'Tab' key and → move the 'active cell' to the right. So use the 'Enter' key or ↓ when you are working down columns and 'Tab' key or → when going across rows to enter your text.

How do I ...?

Input text

Text which is wider than the column will flow over into the next cell if this is empty, as in the heading 'FINANCIAL FORECAST'. When you are keying-in text into the following cell, the text in the previous cell is partly hidden (this is how it will print out). As a result you will need to widen the column to fit the text as in column A (see page 53).

	A	B	C	D
1	FINANCIAL FORECAST			
2				
3		January	February	March
4	Housekee⌐	600	600	600
5				

Never leave blank columns. Always change the width as necessary to display your data.

The text automatically lines up to the left of the column unless you change this (see page 60).

How do I ...?

Correct data while keying-in

When you key-in text, a flashing vertical cursor appears following the first keystroke in the 'active cell'. However, your data is not 'entered' into the cell until you press another key (see page 36). To delete text before 'entering' it into a cell, **position** the mouse pointer, which looks like aḣ (I-beam)**,** next to the mistake, **click** the left mouse button and **press** one of the following keys.

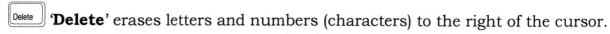

'**Delete**' erases letters and numbers (characters) to the right of the cursor.

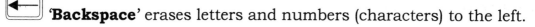

'**Backspace**' erases letters and numbers (characters) to the left.

Or, to quickly remove all the contents of the cell **press 'Esc'** or, **click** on the 'Cancel' X button on the 'formula bar'. When you key-in text, it appears on the 'formula bar' as well as in the 'active cell'. **Position** the I-beam next to the mistake on the 'formula bar' and **click** to make corrections there.

Information Technology Resources – User Guide for Excel 97
© ITR 1999

How do I ...?

Make corrections and edit data

When you have 'entered' data into a cell, you can replace or edit it. To change the entire contents of the cell, **click** on the cell and **key-in** the correction and then **'enter'** the new version.

To edit part of the cell contents, **press F2** (see page 15) and the cursor is placed to the right of the data to allow you to make changes easily. Or, **click** on the cell and its contents appear on the 'formula bar'. **Position** the mouse pointer (I-beam) on the 'formula bar' where you are going to make the correction and **click** the left mouse button. Use the delete keys to erase unwanted letters or numbers.

To change an entire word, **double click** anywhere within the word and the whole word is 'selected'. Once you have 'selected' a word, you do not need to delete it, just **key-in** the replacement and this will type over the highlighted text.

Use **'Ctrl H'** or **'Edit'**, **'Replace'** and **key-in** the data to find, and **key-in** the replacement data. **Click** on 'Find Next' and 'Replace' to individually change data, or 'Replace All' for an automatic replacement. **Click** on 'Close'.

How do I ...?

Undo or Redo a function

Click on the 'Undo' button. This button allows you to reverse (undo) the last function you carried out.

Click on the down arrow at the side of the 'Undo' button to drop down a list of actions. If you need to undo several functions, **drag** over them until the actions are highlighted and then **click** inside the highlighting. You will then undo all those actions.

If you undo something by mistake, **click** on the 'Redo' button.

Do not worry if everything on screen seems to go wrong, 'Undo' can easily take you back to how the spreadsheet was – so don't be afraid of experimenting.

Information Technology Resources – User Guide for Excel 97
© ITR 1999

How do I ...?

<u>AutoCorrect</u>

AutoCorrect automatically corrects your text as you are keying-in. It will correct the following.

Two initial capital letters, for example, THe.
If you accidentally use cAPS LOCK, it corrects the mistake then turns 'Caps Lock' off.
If the first letter after a full stop is lower case, it changes to a capital letter.
If the first letter of a weekday is lower case, it changes to a capital.

It also corrects many common keying-in errors, for example, 'teh' with 'the'. You can add words to 'AutoCorrect' to cater for your own needs. To do this, **click** on **'Tools', 'AutoCorrect'** and **key-in** the wrongly-spelled word in the 'Replace:' box. **Key-in** the correct version in the 'With:' box and **click** on **'Add'**. You can delete entries in the same way. Note the list of 'AutoCorrect' entries and see how you can quickly insert symbols into documents using this feature.

How do I ...?

<u>Use AutoComplete</u>

Excel compares any new text you are keying-in with existing entries in that column. If the first few characters are the same as a previous entry, it will complete your cell automatically. To accept this, **press 'Enter'**. Or, continue keying-in your data and the highlighted letters will disappear and be replaced by your entry. To delete unwanted characters that have been entered automatically, **press 'Backspace'**.

Or, **press 'Alt'** ↓ to drop down a list of items already keyed-in that column. **Click** on the entry you need. Or, **click** the right mouse button and **click** 'Pick from List' on the 'shortcut menu'.

AutoComplete only applies to text or text and numbers. Numbers, dates and time will not be completed.

To turn off this feature, **click 'Tools', 'Options', 'Edit'** and **click** 'Enable AutoComplete for cell values'.

How do I ...?

Use AutoCalculate

It is possible to work out the value of a range of cells without using a formula.

Drag over the range of cells and its total value will be displayed on the 'status bar' (see pages 12 and 13).

You can also perform other calculations. **Click** with the right mouse button on the 'status bar' to display this 'shortcut menu'. **Click** on **'Average'**. This will produce an average of all the cells in the range.

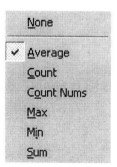

How do I ...?

<u>Spellcheck my work</u>

Click on the 'Spelling' 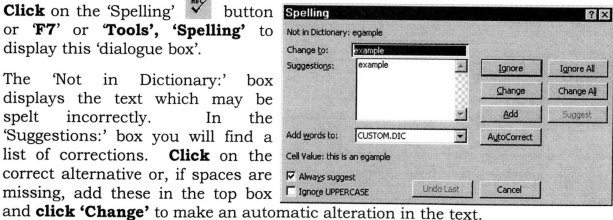 button or **'F7'** or **'Tools', 'Spelling'** to display this 'dialogue box'.

The 'Not in Dictionary:' box displays the text which may be spelt incorrectly. In the 'Suggestions:' box you will find a list of corrections. **Click** on the correct alternative or, if spaces are missing, add these in the top box and **click 'Change'** to make an automatic alteration in the text.

Remember 'Spellcheck' will not always recognise words – especially names – so treat the suggested corrections with some caution. If you know the spellings are correct, **click** on **'Ignore'** to bypass the word or name once or **'Ignore All'** for the whole document.

How do I ...?

<u>Insert a formula</u>

You use formulae using cell references, not cell contents, in spreadsheets to make calculations (see page 25). The formulae will automatically update calculations when you change related cell contents.

Every formula always begins with an equals (=) sign. To add together the numbers in the cells 'B5' and 'B6' and place the answer in cell 'B7', the formula in cell 'B7' would be **=B5+B6**. If you made changes to the numbers in 'B5' or 'B6', the answer in 'B7' would be changed. The answer to the formula is shown in the cell, and the formula is displayed on the 'formula bar' when you select the cell. You can choose to display all the formulae in a spreadsheet (see page 46). The symbols used in formulae are shown below.

+   addition, for example **=C3+D29**
-      subtraction, for example **=B5-C5**
*   multiplication, for example **=C6*D6**
/   division, for example **=F7/E7**
%   percentage, for example **=17.5%*D2**
^   exponents, for example **=2^2** is 2 raised to the power of 2

How do I ...?

Display formulae in the spreadsheet

What you produce from the formula is shown in the cell. However, you can display the formulae used.

Hold down 'Ctrl' key and **press** ` to display formulae on screen. Or, **click** on **'Tools', 'Options', 'View'** and **click** under 'Window options' on the 'Formulas' box.

How the text is aligned on the screen will be different. This is normal when you view formulae and you cannot change this alignment. If this has to be printed out, see page 91 for options on fitting to one page.

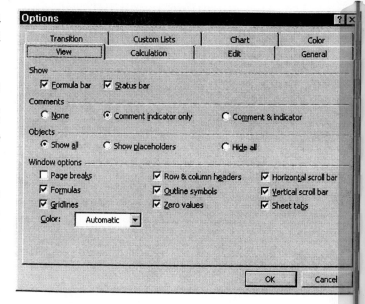

46

How do I ...?

Insert date and time

To insert the date, **key-in** the following formula.

=today()

Remember to use an open and closing bracket after the word 'today'. Or, **press 'Ctrl ;'**

To insert both the date and time, **key-in** the following formula.

=now()

You can change the way that the date is shown by formatting the cells (see pages 81 and 82).

How do I ...?

<u>Use the SUM function</u>

The SUM function adds up cells in a range you have selected. It would take a lot of time to input, for example, **=B3+B4+B5+B6+B7+B8**. Excel contains shortcuts (functions) you can use when you want to build formulae. You could add this range of cells together using the SUM function. It would then read **=SUM(B3:B8)**.

Click on the cell where the answer to the sum is to appear. **Key-in '=SUM('** then **click** on the first cell in the range. In the example above that is 'B3', then **hold down** the mouse button and **drag** over the rest of the range. A shimmering line appears round the cells you want to add together. The number of rows and columns you have selected is shown as you drag over the cells (6R x 1C). **Press 'Enter'** or **click** on the 'Enter' button on the 'formula bar'. You will see the answer to the calculation in the cell, but the formula is shown on the 'formula bar'. You can now copy this formula into other cells (see page 68).

Notice that Excel uses a colon (:) between the cell numbers. You can key-in the whole formula yourself if you want rather than using the mouse. Remember to key-in **'=function name('** before choosing the range.

How do I ...?

Use AutoSum

The SUM function is the one you will most often use in Excel. To make this operation easier, you can use the 'AutoSum' function. Whenever you want to add up a range of cells, **click** in the cell where you want the answer to appear and **click** on the 'AutoSum' Σ button. Excel puts a shimmering line round the range of cells which it thinks you want to add together. If this is correct, **press 'Enter'** or **click** on the 'Enter' button. If the suggested range is not correct, **click** and **drag** over the cells you want to add together or, **key-in** the changes, and 'Enter' this formula.

If you position the 'active cell' at the bottom of a column of figures, Excel will assume you want to add up all the column. If you place the 'active cell' at the end of a row of numbers, Excel will assume you want to add the row together.

To make sure you get a correct result, you can **select** the range of cells you want to work with first and then **click** on the 'AutoSum' button.

How do I ...?

Further functions

You can use other functions for calculations on a range or cells in the same way as the SUM function (see page 48). Some examples are given below or see page 49.

Average	This is the average of all the values in the range **=Average(B3:B8)**
Count	This counts the number of items of data in the range, (it does not includes empty cells and text) **=Count(B3:B8)**
CountA	This counts all the items in a range except empty cells **=CountA(B3:B8)**
Max	This is the largest value in the range **=Max(B3:B8)**
Min	This is the smallest value in the range **=Min(B3:B8)**
Sqrt	This gives the square root of a number or cell **=sqrt(B3)** or **=sqrt(25)** (This only works for positive numbers not negative ones).

Information Technology Resources – User Guide for Excel 97
© ITR 1999

How do I ...?

Use the Paste Function button

Another way of inserting a function is by using the 'Paste Function' button. **Select** the cell you want to contain the formula and then **click** on the 'Paste Function' f_∞ button to display this 'dialogue box'.

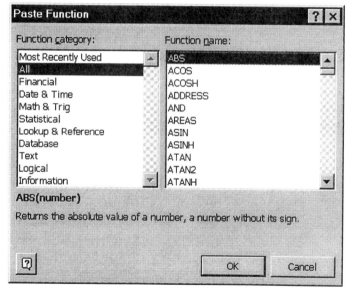

Click on a category and scroll through the function names on the right. **Double click** on the one you want. The suggested range is then shown. To change this, **click** on the 'Collapse' button to hide the 'dialogue box' and **drag** over the new range. **Click** on the 'Expand' button or **'Enter'** to display the 'dialogue box' and **click** on **'OK'**.

How do I ...?

<u>Use the Edit Formula button</u>

Select the cell for the formula. **Click** on the 'Edit Formula' = button. The Formula Bar changes as shown below.

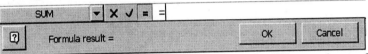

Click on **'SUM'** if that is correct, or **click** on the ▼ to show further functions. The screen then shows the suggested range.

Click on the 'Collapse' button to hide the 'dialogue box' and **drag** over the new range. **Click** on the 'Expand' button or **'Enter'** to display the 'dialogue box' and **click** on **'OK'**. Or, you can **key-in** the correct range.

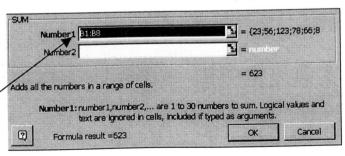

How do I ...?

Change the width of columns

If you key-in a number (not text) which is wider than the column, the column will automatically widen to fit that number. If you have reset the width of the column yourself, the number would appear as '#####' (see page 28). Increase the size of the column to show the full number. To change the width of columns, see below.

Point to the vertical line between the column letters and the mouse pointer changes to ◀┃▶. **Click** and **drag** the line to its new position. Or, you can **double click** on the vertical line and the column will change to fit in the longest line.

Or, you can select a cell in a column or a range of cells or **click** on the **'Select All'** button or **'Ctrl A'**, **click** on **'Format'**, **'Column'** **'Width'** to display this 'dialogue box'. **Key-in** a number and you will have changed all the columns in the range.

How do I ...?

<u>Save a new workbook</u>

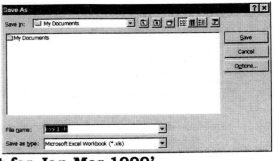

Click on the 'Save' button or **'Ctrl s'** or **'File'**, **'Save'** to display this 'dialogue box'.

Each time Excel begins a new workbook, it is automatically named on the title bar as 'Book' followed by a number. When you are saving the document, use a meaningful name. File names can be up to 255 letters or numbers and spaces, for example **'Budget for Jan-Mar 1999'**.

Excel puts the suggested name in the 'File name:' box. While it is still highlighted, **key-in** the name you want and then check in the 'Save in:' box to make sure you are saving it to the correct drive and folder (see pages 29 and 30). Use the **'Up One Level'** button to move through the folders. Or, you can create a new folder to hold your spreadsheets. To do this **click** on the 'Create New Folder' button and at the 'New Folder' 'dialogue box' **key-in** the name for the folder and **click** on **'OK'**.

How do I ...?

<u>Save an existing document</u>

The 'title bar' at the top of the screen will display the name of a workbook you have already saved.

To save the workbook with the same file name **click** on the 'Save' button or **'Ctrl s'** or **'File', 'Save'**. This will save any changes you have made to the document and overwrite the original file.

If you want to have 2 versions of the file, your original and the second with a different file name, **press** (Function key) **'F12'** or **'File', 'Save As'**. You then have the chance to name your second version with a different file name.

You can save workbooks as different types. Excel automatically creates files which end in **'.xls'**. However, you can save files in different formats, **click** on the arrow alongside the 'Save as type:' box and choose another format.

How do I ...?

<u>Print Preview</u>

Click on the 'Print Preview'  button or **'File'**, **'Print Preview'** before you print any document to check its layout. Print Preview shows the layout on the page.

A small version of the whole page is shown which does not allow you to read the data, but just check the layout. When the cursor is over the text, the pointer becomes a magnifying glass. **Click** on this and that part of the data is enlarged. **Click** again to see the full page.

To see other pages, **click** on 'Next' button on the 'print preview toolbar'. To return to the previous page, **click** on 'Previous' button.

| Next | Previous | Zoom | Print... | Setup... | Margins | Page Break Preview | Close | Help |

To return to the normal screen **click** on the 'Close' | Close | button on the 'print preview toolbar'.

How do I ...?

Print a workbook

Click on the 'Print' 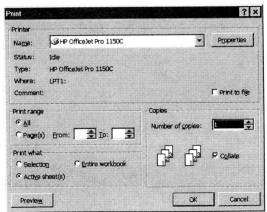 button if you want to print without choosing any options.

For printer options, **press 'Ctrl P'** or **click** on **'File'**, **'Print'** to display the 'dialogue box'. Under 'Print range', choose either **'All'** (the whole workbook) **'Pages'** and **key-in** the page numbers. Or, under 'Print what' **click** on **'Selection'** to print selected cells or **'Active sheet'** for the sheet where you place the cursor.

If you want many copies, **key-in** the number you need under 'Copies'. To change the printer, **click** on ▼ alongside 'Name:' and make your choice.

Or, to print files which are not open, **click** on the file names at the 'Open' 'dialogue box' (see page 33), **press** the right mouse button and **click** on **'Print'**.

How do I ...?

Print selected areas

Always make sure that you place the 'active cell' inside the data you want printed. Sometimes you can print out blank columns and rows as a result of the 'active cell' being in the wrong position.

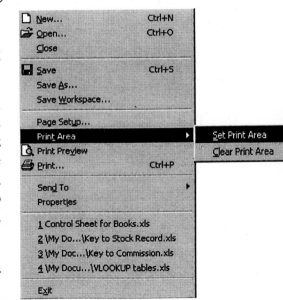

To overcome this problem, you can select an area you want to print. **Drag** over the cells you want to print. **Click** on **'File'**, **'Print Area'** and **'Set Print Area'**. **Click** outside the selection and you will see a dotted line around the print area. **Print** in the usual way. To remove this selection, **'File'**, **'Print Area'**, **'Clear Print Area'**.

This is useful if you want to print cells you have selected within a worksheet.

How do I ...?

<u>Close a workbook or Excel</u>

Click on the 'Close' ☒ button on the 'menu bar' or **'Ctrl W'** or **'Ctrl F4'** or **'File', 'Close'**.

The screen prompt may ask you if you want to save the changes. This is a reminder and you should usually answer **'Yes'**.

To close all open workbooks without leaving Excel, **hold down** the **'Shift'** key, and **click** on **'File', 'Close All'**.

To close Excel **click** on the 'Close' button on the 'title bar' or **'File', 'Exit'**.

To close all open documents and leave Excel, **press 'Alt F4'**. The computer will ask you if you want to save your work.

How do I ...?

<u>Align data</u>

Text normally lines up at the left of a column and numbers at the right, but you can change this. The 'formatting toolbar' contains 3 buttons for aligning text.

 Align Left – This is when text and numbers start at the left of the column.

 Centre – This is when every line is centred over the column.

 Align Right – This is when the text and numbers line up at the right of the column.

You can 'select' an individual cell, **click** on it and change how it is aligned. Or, you can 'select' a range of cells (see page 23) and change their alignment all at the same time.

Remember if text is too long to fit the width of the column, it will not all show. See page 53 on how to widen columns to display all text and numbers. You should leave numbers and change text over numbers so they are aligned to the right.

How do I ...?

Centre headings over cells

The alignment buttons are useful if you want to change the format of cells, rows or columns. However, you may want to centre a heading over several columns or a range of cells.

Key-in the text in the first cell of the range over which you want the heading to be centred. **Click** in this cell and **drag** across the cells which the heading is to be centred over.

When you have done this, **click** on the 'Merge and Centre' button. The cells which you 'selected' are merged together and the heading will be centred within this one cell.

How do I ...?

Emphasise data

You can emphasise text or numbers by using the 'Bold', 'Italic' and 'Underline' features.

To change one word, **move** the cursor inside the word and **click** on the button you need on the 'formatting toolbar'. To change more than one word, **select** the text first. To change a whole row or column 'select' the row or column title before you **click** on the appropriate button. To change cells which are not next to each other, **hold down** the '**Ctrl**' key and **click** on each cell.

B   or '**Ctrl B**'   **Bold** – the printing is darker.

I   or '**Ctrl I**'   *Italic* - the letters have a sloping, handwritten appearance.

U   or '**Ctrl U**'   Underline – the data is underlined.

To repeat the formatting, **press 'F4'**. To remove formatting **select** the data and **click** the format button again or, **click** on '**Edit**', '**Clear**', '**Formats**'.

How do I ...?

<u>Change the font</u>

The font is the appearance of the printed data and the variety of fonts available depends on the software installed on your computer. **Select** the cells you want to change and **Click** on the 'Font' and 'Font Size' Arial ▼ 10 ▼ buttons on the 'formatting toolbar' or **click** on **'Format'**, **'Cells'** and **click** on the 'Font' tab to show this 'dialogue box'. You can choose different fonts, styles, sizes, underlining and colours. Anything you choose will be shown in the 'Preview' box.

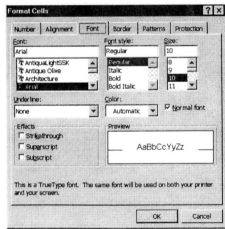

If the cells you are changing are not next to each other, **hold down** the 'Ctrl' key while you **click** on each cell to 'select' it.

You can colour text by clicking on the 'Font Colour' button.

How do I ...?

<u>Use Format Painter</u>

If you want to copy several formatting options from one cell to another, use the Format Painter. For copying just one format, for example, bold, use the **'F4'** key (see page 12).

Click on the cell where you have already used the formatting, for example, font, colour, size, bold, italics or underscore (see pages 62 and 63). **Click** on the 'Format Painter' button on the 'standard toolbar'. As you move the mouse pointer onto the worksheet you will see it has a paintbrush attached to it.

Click on the cell to which you want the formatting to apply.

Format Painter will only work once. If you need to change more than one cell, **drag** across the range of cells with the paintbrush. If you need to make other changes, you will need to **click** on Format Painter again.

How do I ...?

Use AutoFormat

You can quickly and easily improve the appearance of your spreadsheet by choosing an AutoFormat.

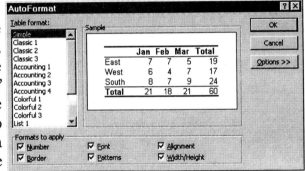

Select the range of cells you want to be formatted. **Click** on **'Format'**, **'AutoFormat'** to display this 'dialogue box'. **Select** a different 'Table format:' and note the 'Sample' you have displayed. **Click** on **'Options >>'** to show the 'Formats to apply'. **Click** on **'Width/Height'** to keep the original size of rows and columns. Experiment with the various options. **Click** on **'OK'** when you have made your choice and this layout will then apply to your spreadsheet.

To remove an AutoFormat, **click** on **'Format'**, **'AutoFormat'** and **select 'None'** from the bottom of the list of styles.

How do I ...?

Move data and cut and paste

Select the cells you want to move. **Click** on the 'Cut' ✂ button or '**Ctrl X**' or '**Edit**', '**Cut**' or **click** on the right mouse button for the 'shortcut menu' and **click** on '**Cut**'. A shimmering line appears round the cells you have chosen. **Move** the mouse pointer to the first cell of the new position and **press 'Enter'** or **click** on the 'Paste' 📋 button or '**Ctrl V**' or '**Edit**', '**Paste**' or '**Paste**' on the 'shortcut menu'. The cells are moved to that position. Any existing data is then overwritten.

✂ Cut
📋 Copy
📋 Paste
Paste Special...
Insert...
Delete...
Clear Contents
📝 Insert Comment
📝 Format Cells...
Pick From List...

Or, **select** the cells and **point** at the border round the cells you have chosen and the mouse pointer changes to a ↖. **Click** and **hold down** the left mouse button and **drag** the cells to their new position. This is called 'drag and drop'.

Items which you 'cut' are placed in Excel's short-term memory called the 'Clipboard' hence the picture of a clipboard on the 'Paste' button. You can copy data into the same worksheet, onto other worksheets, into other workbooks or into other applications, for example 'Word', by using the clipboard.

How do I ...?

Copy data

Select the cells and **click** on the 'Copy' button or **'Ctrl C'** or **'Edit'**, **'Copy'**. Or, you can **click** on **'Copy'** from the 'shortcut menu'. A shimmering line is shown around the cell or cells.

Move the mouse pointer to the new position and **press 'Enter'** or **click** on the 'Paste' button or **'Ctrl V'** or **'Edit'**, **'Paste'** or **click 'Paste'** on the 'shortcut menu'. The data will then be copied to that place. You now have your original data and a copy of it.

Once you have stored an item on the 'Clipboard', you can paste it in as many times as you need, as long as you use the 'Paste' command. If you use 'Enter' to input the copy, you can only copy the data once.

Or, you can **drag and drop** the cells (see page 66). However, **hold down** the 'Ctrl' key to make sure you copy the cells and not move them. You can copy data to other software applications (see page 99).

How do I ...?

Copy formulae or data

When you copy text and individual numbers, they stay the same. However, when you copy formulae Excel changes them to make them 'relate' to the row or column they are copied into.

If you copy the formula **=A1+B1** from cell 'C1' into cells 'C2' and 'C3', it will change with each row as

	A	B	C
1	3	4	=A1+B1
2	7	8	=A2+B2
3	5	7	=A3+B3

shown. The formula is now 'relative' to the row it is in – in other words it now has the same row number.

To copy a formula, **click** on the cell containing the formula and **point** at the 'fill handle' (see page 12) a small square at the bottom right corner of the cell. The mouse pointer changes to a **+**. **Click** and **drag** over the cells you want to 'fill'. The formulae will automatically change with each new row.

You can use this technique for formulae or for text and for single cells containing numbers either across, up or down the worksheet. It will only change formulae.

How do I ...?

Create a series

You can use the 'fill handle' (see page 14) for copying, but it also allows you to produce the days of the week, months and so on without keying-in.

Key-in 'Mon', and **'Enter'** it. **Click** on the cell and using the 'fill handle' **+**, **drag** either up or down the column or across the row in any direction. Excel automatically enters the other days of the week in their abbreviated form. If you had keyed-in 'Monday' Excel would have put the days out in full.

Other text which you can use in this way is shown below.

Jan or January   21/04/99 (dates)
1st Quarter   selected cells containing numbers

As you drag, a small box appears to tell you where you are up to in the series. A single number will not produce a series, but if you key-in numbers into 2 cells and **select** both cells then **drag** using the 'fill handle', Excel will then continue the number series.

You can add your own custom list. **Click 'Tools', 'Options', 'Custom Lists'** and **click** on **'NEW LIST'**. **Key-in** the data you need, **click** on **'Add'** and **'OK'**.

How do I ...?

<u>Copy items not in a series</u>

You may want to insert the same date for several items. If you use the 'fill handle', it would produce consecutive dates.

Key-in the date in the first cell. **Click** on the date and **click** on the 'Copy' button. Or, you can **click** with the right mouse button for 'shortcut menu' and **click** on '**Copy**' or '**Ctrl C**' or '**Edit**', '**Copy**'. A shimmering line appears around the cell. Using the ⊡ mouse pointer, **select** the cells into which you want to copy the date - the shimmering line will stay around the first cell – **press** '**Enter**' or **click** on '**Paste**'.

You can also use the 'Ctrl' key and the 'fill handle' (a smaller + is added to the 'fill handle') to copy the date into a range of cells. To copy the same date into cells which are not next to each other**, click** on the date, **hold down** the 'Ctrl' key, **point** at the 'cell border'. The mouse pointer will change to an arrow with the smaller cross attached. **Drag** this to the new position.

How do I ...?

Copy formulae into rows which are not next to each other

The 'fill handle' is useful when you are copying formulae to cells which are placed together. However, you can copy a formula to individual cells.

Click on the cell containing the formula and **click** on the 'Copy' button. Or, you can **'Copy'** from the 'shortcut' menu or **'Ctrl C'** or **'Edit', 'Copy'**. **Click** on the new cell for the formula and **click** on the **'Paste'** button, or **'Ctrl V'** or **'Edit', 'Paste'**. The formula you have copied will carry out the same function as it did before, but the cell references will now be 'relative' to the new row or column (see page 68).

Or, you can **select** the cell containing the formula, **hold down** the 'Ctrl' key and **point** with the mouse at the cell. When the mouse pointer changes to an arrow, **drag** the formula to its new position.

How do I ...?

Deal with circular references

A 'circular reference' is a formula containing the cell reference of the 'active cell'. Excel will find the 'circular reference' and may show an error message.

If you know you have made a mistake, **click** on **'OK'** and correct your formula. If you are not sure where the mistake is, check the Status Bar and you will see a reference to the cell containing the faulty formula. The cell itself may contain a blue dot.

The 'Circular Reference toolbar' should be displayed, if not see page 19. **Click** on the ▼ to 'drop down' a list of cells you believe the mistake could be in. **Click** on the 'Trace Precedents' button and a blue line appears to show the cells which the formula

applies to. **Click** on that cell and check and edit the formula as you need to. If you need a circular reference, **click** on **'Tools'**, **'Options'**, **'Calculation'** and **click** on **'Iteration'**. You can then set the number and degree of change you need.

How do I ...?

<u>Centre the spreadsheet on the page</u>

When in 'Print Preview' you can change the layout of your spreadsheet on the page. **Click** on 'Print Preview' button (see page 56) and **click** on 'Setup ...' button.

Click on the 'Margins' tab to display this 'dialogue box'. **Click** under 'Centre on page' to centre the spreadsheet horizontally or vertically on the page. Notice the page layout changes to show your choices. **Click** on **'OK'**.

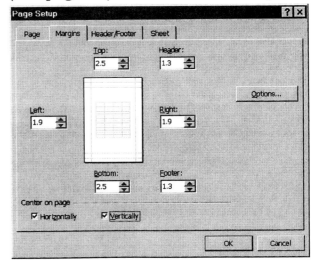

How do I ...?

Change paper to landscape

Excel will always print out spreadsheets on portrait paper (with the shorter edge at the top) unless you change this setting.

Click 'File', 'Page Setup' and **click** the 'Page' tab to display this 'dialogue box'. **Click** on **'Landscape'**.

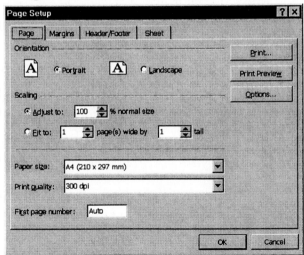

You can also make your spreadsheet fit onto a single page (see page 91), **choose** different paper sizes and print quality.

Click on 'Print Preview' to see your changes before you print them.

Or, you can use **'Print Preview'** and **'Setup ...'** to change the setting.

How do I ...?

<u>Change text within cells</u>

Select the cell or cells you want to change. **Press 'Ctrl 1'** or **click** on **'Format', 'Cells'** and **click** on the 'Alignment' tab to display this 'dialogue box'.

To make text wrap round in a cell, **click** on the 'Wrap text' box. The cell is then made longer to allow you to see the text fully. Widening the column will change how the text appears. Or, **press 'Alt' 'Enter'** to begin a new line within the cell.

You can display text vertically or at an angle. **Click** on the 'Orientation' option. Or, to place it at any angle, **click** on the 'Degrees' box. Experiment with different options and 'Undo' if you need to.

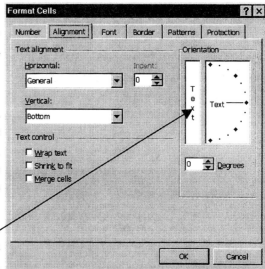

How do I ...?

Inset text in a cell

You can inset text from the left of the cell. You can **select** the cell or range of cells and **click** on the 'Increase Indent' button on the 'formatting toolbar'. This will move the text in one space each time you click it.

To remove an indent, **select** the cell and **click** on the 'Decrease Indent' button.

Or, you can use **'Ctrl 1'** or **'Format'**, **'Cells'**, **'Alignment'** and under 'Horizontal:' **select 'Left (Indent)'**. Then **click** on the **'Indent'** box to show the number of spaces to move the text in from the left of the cell.

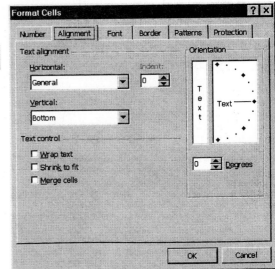

76

How do I ...?

Insert or delete columns and rows

Click inside the column to the right of where you want to add the new column. **Click** on **'Insert' 'Columns'** and a new column is inserted to the left of the 'active cell'. It will also be given the letter of that column. Any formulae will include the new column. Or, **click** the right mouse button to show this 'shortcut menu'. **Click** on **'Insert'** and the 'Insert' menu appears. **Click** on **'Entire column'** and **'OK'**. To add several columns, **drag** across that number of cells and 'Insert' as above. That number of columns will be inserted to the left of the columns you have chosen.

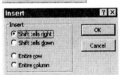

To add new rows, **position** the 'active cell' in the row below where you want to insert the blanks. You can then insert as shown above. To add many rows, **drag** over the number you need below the point where you want them before you **click** on **'Insert'**. Always check formulae after inserting columns and rows.

To delete columns and rows, **select** and **click** on **'Delete'** from the shortcut menu. **'Clear Contents'** erases the contents, but not the column or row.

How do I ...?

Insert a range of cells

You will find the method of inserting columns and rows in page 77 affects the whole spreadsheet. If you want to add blank cells by moving other cells, you can do this easily and it will only change the range you have chosen.

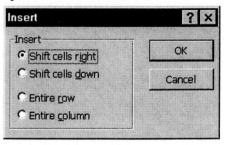

Select the range of cells you want to move. **Click** the right mouse button to show the 'shortcut menu' and **click** on **'Insert'** to show this 'dialogue box'. If you choose to insert 'Entire row' or 'Entire column', this will add the same number of row or columns that you chose.

Or, you can choose to 'Shift cells right' or 'Shift cells down'. The highlighted cells will move by the number of columns or rows you have chosen. Remember if the cells are blank they will appear not to change. You can also move a range of cells to any place by using 'drag and drop' (see page 66).

How do I ...?

<u>Delete a range of cells</u>

If you want to erase the contents of cells, **select** the cells and **press 'Delete'**. Or, you can **click** the right mouse button for the 'shortcut menu' and **click** on **'Clear Contents'**.

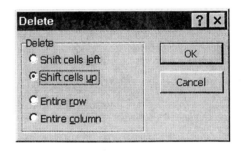

If you want to remove the cells as well as their contents, **select** the range of cells, **click** on the right mouse button. **Click** on **'Delete'** on the 'shortcut menu' to show this 'dialogue box'.

You can choose to delete an 'Entire row' or 'Entire column' to erase the rows and columns that the cells are in. Or, you can delete the cells and move the existing cells either up or to the left.

How do I ...?

Increase or decrease the number of decimal places

Select the cells containing the numbers. **Click** on the 'Increase Decimal' button on the 'formatting toolbar' to make sure the numbers all have the same number of decimal places.

Then **click** on the 'Increase Decimal' button again for more places or **click** on the 'Decrease Decimal' button to reduce the number of decimal places. Or, you can make the numbers into 'Integer' format, that is whole numbers (no decimal places).

With whole numbers, any figure with a decimal place below **.45** is rounded down to the number below. Any number which has a decimal place of **.45** or above is taken to the number above. Remember that this happens as the original number will be used in calculations and may affect the totals in your spreadsheet.

Information Technology Resources – User Guide for Excel 97
© ITR 1999

How do I ...?

Format cells as numbers or currency

Select the column, row or range of cells you want to format and **press 'Ctrl 1'**. Or, you can **click** with the right mouse button to show 'shortcut menu' and **click** on **'Format Cells'** or **pull down 'Format'**, **'Cells'** to display this 'dialogue box'.

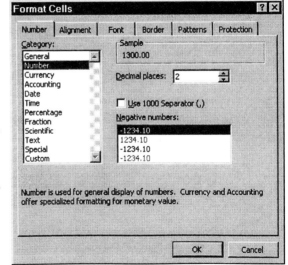

You can display figures in a number of different ways as listed under 'Category:'. **Click** on each one to see the options available. These are shown at the right of the box.

If your data is not displayed as you would expect, always check the format of the cells is correct, for example $5.00 for currency (£5). **Select** 'Currency' and 'Symbol' to change to a £.

How do I ...?

Select a custom format for numbers

If the format you want is not shown in the appropriate category, you can choose a 'Custom' format. Open the 'dialogue box' (see page 81) and with the 'Number' tab at the front, **click** on 'Custom'.

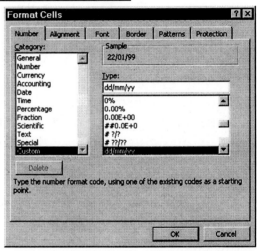

Scroll through the options available. You can change the way that data is displayed, for example, you can show the date as:

24/04/99 or **24-Apr-99** or **24-Apr** or **Apr-99**. However, watch out for American dates where the month is shown first.

To create your own custom format, see Excel's Help Index, **'Contents and Index'**, **'Index'**, **'Customizing'**, **'Number formats'**, **'Create a custom number format'**.

How do I ...?

<u>Use the toolbar buttons for number formats</u>

These 3 buttons are on the 'formatting toolbar' and can make formatting cells quicker.

Currency – the £ is shown at the left of the column and the numbers line up at the right. Use **'Ctrl' 'Shift' '$'** to keep £ with numbers or use **'Format' 'Cells'**. All these will display 2 decimal places.

Percent style – shows numbers as percentages. You may still need to use the 'Increase Decimal' button.

Comma style – commas will be inserted to separate thousands and 2 decimal places will be shown.

How do I ...?

<u>Add borders and coloured lines to cells</u>

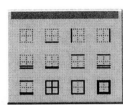

Select the cell or range of cells which you want to add the border to and **click** on ▼ beside the 'Borders ⊞ · button to display this 'drop-down box'. **Click** on the border you want.

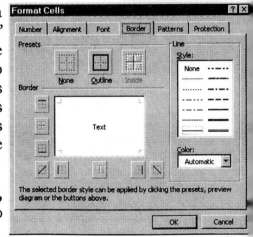

For more choice, **press 'Ctrl 1'** or **click** on **'Format', 'Cells' 'Border'. Click** on a 'Preset' format or use the 'Style:' box to choose a line option. You can then choose your line 'Colour' to create your own format. **Click** on the buttons under 'Border' to put lines on and take them off as you need. You can even add diagonal lines in this way. **Click** on **'OK'**. Remember to click outside the highlighting to see the results of the formatting.

To clear formats, **select** the cell or cells and **'Edit', 'Clear' 'Formats'**. Or, you can **select** the 'No border' option on the 'Borders' button.

Information Technology Resources – User Guide for Excel 97

How do I ...?

Fill a cell with colour

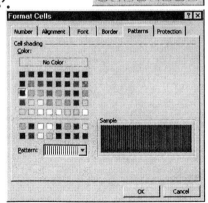

Select a cell or range of cells to which you want to add colour and **click** on ▼ beside the 'Fill Colour' 🪣 ▾ button. This will display this 'drop-down box'. **Click** on the colour you want.

For more choice, **click** on **'Format', 'Cells' 'Patterns'.** **Choose** a colour and it is shown in the 'Sample' box.

To add a pattern to your colour, **click** on ▼ beside 'Pattern:' and you will see a choice of colours and patterns. **Select** a pattern and see the change in the 'Sample' box. You can also choose a pattern colour which will mix with your original colour to create a different effect. Experiment! If you no longer want a pattern, **click** on **'No Colour'**.

To remove a colour from a cell or cells **click** on ▼ beside 'Fill Colour' and **click** on **'No Fill'**.

How do I ...?

<u>Insert and delete pre-set headers and footers</u>

There are several ways of opening this 'dialogue box'. **Click** on **'View'**, **'Header and Footer'** or **'File', 'Page Setup'** and make sure the 'Header and Footer' tab is at the front.

Or, you can insert headers and footers while you are looking at your document. **Click** on the 'Print Preview' button and **click** on 'Setup'. Make sure the 'Header and Footer' tab is at the front.

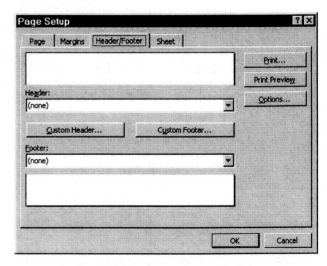

Click on the ▼ below 'Header:' or 'Footer:' and choose one of the pre-set options. **Select (none)** to remove the header or footer.

How do I ...?

Insert and delete customised headers and footers

At the 'Page Setup' 'dialogue box' with 'Header and Footer' tab at the front, **click** on **'Custom Header'** or **'Custom Footer'** to show this 'dialogue box'.

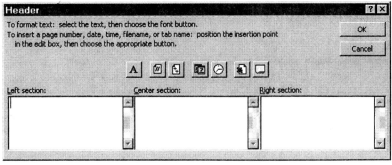

Key-in your text in the 'Left section:' and **press 'Tab'** key to move to the 'Centre section:'. Whatever you key-in here will be centred between the margins. **Press 'Tab'** key to move to 'Right section:' (text is right-aligned). You can format your text or insert items with the buttons. They are as follows.

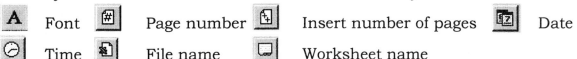

A Font   Page number   Insert number of pages   Date

Time   File name   Worksheet name

To remove a header or footer, **select** the text and **press 'Delete'**.

How do I ...?

<u>Change margins 1</u>

Click on **'File'**, **'Page Setup'** to show the 'dialogue box'. Make sure that the 'Margins' tab is at the front. Use the 'Tab' key to move through the margin boxes. When a number is highlighted, you can key over the top. You do not need to delete anything.

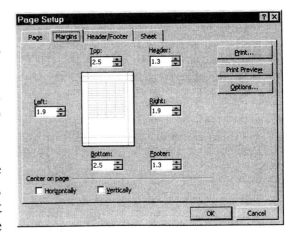

The normal margins for Excel are 2.5 centimetres (1 inch) top and bottom, 1.9 centimetres (¾ inch) left and right and 1.3 centimetres (½ inch) from the header and footer to the edge of the page.

You can **click** on 'Print Preview' in the 'dialogue box' to see your changes before you print them, or you can **click** on **'Print'**.

How do I ...?

Change margins 2

You can change the margins in 'Print Preview'. **Click** on the 'Print Preview' button and **click** on **'Margins'**. The margins are shown as lines which you can drag around the screen and see your changes immediately.

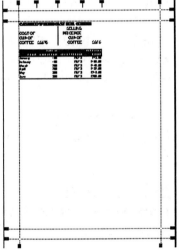

The mouse pointer is a magnifying glass, but when you place it over a vertical line, it changes to **↔** . **Click** and **hold down** and **drag** the margin line to its new position. As you **click** on the line, the size and name of the margin are displayed on the 'status bar'.

To drag a horizontal line, **move** the mouse pointer over the line and it changes to **↕**. The horizontal lines represent the header or footer margin and the top or bottom margin.

How do I ...?

Fit my worksheet onto one page

If your spreadsheet is showing a vertical or horizontal dotted line, this shows that it will not fit on a single sheet of paper.

Click on **'File', 'Page Setup'** or **click** on 'Print Preview button and **click** on 'Page' tab to display this 'dialogue box'.

Under 'Scaling' you can 'Fit to' so you can choose the number of pages for your final printout.

Always check the layout after you have chosen this option, in case page breaks appear in the wrong place.

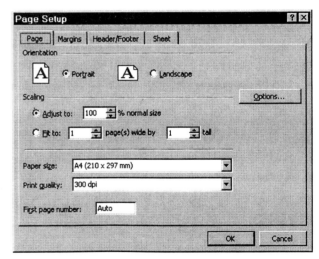

How do I ...?

<u>Insert page breaks</u>

You can change the position of page breaks (see pages 12 and 13) by inserting your own 'hard' page break. For a horizontal page break, **move** the 'active cell' in column A of the row below where you want to begin the next page. **Click** on **'Insert', 'Page Break'**. Excel puts a dotted line to show where the new page will begin. For a vertical page break, **click** on the column heading to the right of where you want the page to break. To remove **click** on **'Insert', 'Remove Page Break'**.

To see the page breaks you have created, **click** on the 'Print Preview' button and you will see the first page of your worksheet. **Click** on the 'Next' or 'Previous' buttons to see the other pages of the document.

Click on 'Page Break Preview' and you will see a smaller version of your spreadsheet with a blue line which shows where your page breaks. **Point** at the line and the pointer becomes a ↕ . **Click** and **drag** this line to move its position. **Click** on **'View', 'Normal'** to return to your worksheet.

Information Technology Resources – User Guide for Excel 97
© ITR 1999

How do I ...?

Insert print titles

You can choose a title, column headings or row headings to appear on each page of your printout. These are called 'print titles'.

Click on **'File', 'Page Setup'** and **click** on the 'Sheet' tab to show this 'dialogue box'. Under 'Print titles' **click** in either rows or columns to repeat this. The cursor appears in the box you have chosen. On the worksheet, **select** the row or column you want to use. **Click** on the blue title bar of 'Page Setup' 'dialogue box' and move it if you need to or, use 'Collapse' and 'Expand' buttons (see page 52). **Click** on **'OK'**.

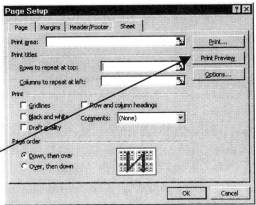

Click on the 'Print Preview' button to see the results of your choice. **Click** on 'Next' button to view extra pages (see page 56). You can change the page order if you need to.

How do I ...?

Print out the gridlines

The standard setting for Excel is that the gridlines will not print out. You can change this if you want.

Click on 'Print Preview' button or **'File', 'Page Setup'** and **click** on the 'Sheet' tab.

Under 'Print' there are several options which allow you to choose to print out the 'Gridlines', or the 'Row and column headings' (the column letters and row numbers). You can also print in black and white only or print in 'Draft quality'.

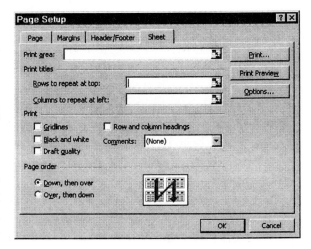

How do I ...?

Add and move worksheets

A new workbook contains 3 worksheets which can each contain many pages. The worksheets appear at the bottom of the screen as 'Sheet 1', 'Sheet 2' and 'Sheet 3'.

| Sheet1 | Sheet2 | Sheet3 |

| Insert... |
| Delete |
| Rename |
| Move or Copy... |
| Select All Sheets |
| View Code |

To add a new worksheet, **click** on **'Insert', 'Worksheet'** and a new sheet (Sheet 4) will be added to the left of the current sheet. Or, **click** on the name tab of the sheet to the right of where you want the page to be made. **Click** the right mouse button for the 'shortcut menu'. **Click** on 'Insert' and **click** on 'Worksheet' at the 'Insert' 'dialogue box'.

To move a worksheet, **click** on its name tab (Sheet 4) and **drag**. The mouse pointer picks up a sheet of paper and small arrow. **Move** the arrow where the sheet is to go and **release** the mouse button.

To copy a worksheet see page 98.

How do I ...?

<u>Delete and rename worksheets</u>

To delete a worksheet, **click** on its name tab. **Click** the right mouse button for the 'shortcut menu' and **'Delete'**. Or, **click** on **'Edit', 'Delete Sheet'**. Excel will display a warning that you will permanently delete the sheet. You can choose to delete the worksheet or cancel the deletion.

To rename a worksheet, **double click** with the left mouse button on its name tab. When you do this you will choose the existing 'Sheet' name. **Key-in** the new name. Or, **click** once with the right mouse button and use the 'shortcut' menu and **click** on **'Rename'**.

How do I ...?

View worksheet name tabs

You may find that you have so many worksheets that you cannot see all their name tabs at the same time.

Use the 'Tab scroll buttons' to scroll and see the name tabs. This does not select the worksheets, it only allows you to see the name tabs.

⏮	Tab scroll to beginning button	◀	Tab scroll left button
⏭	Tab scroll to end button	▶	Tab scroll right button

Or, **find** the 'Tab split box' to the left of the 'horizontal' scroll bar.

⏮ ◀ ▶ ⏭ \ Absolute \ **Selling Price 80p** / MayJune Increase / July Increase / ◀

Click on this box and the cursor changes to the double-headed arrow ◀╫▶ **drag** this to the right to reveal more name tabs.

How do I ...?

<u>Copy a worksheet</u>

To copy a worksheet, **click** on the 'Sheet tab', **hold down** the 'Ctrl' key and **drag**. The mouse pointer has a sheet of paper with a + sign displayed and ▼ attached to it. **Move** the ▼ to the left of the sheet tab where you want to insert the copy. The new sheet will keep the name of the original but with a number added in brackets. You can copy several sheets together in this way. Or, **point** to the 'Sheet tab' and **click** the right mouse button to show this menu. **Click** on **'Move or Copy ...'** to display this 'dialogue box'. **Click** on **'Create a copy'** and **select** the sheet number.

Or, if you need to copy the sheet to a new workbook, **click** on the ▼ alongside 'To book:' and **click** on **'(new book)'**.

Always check formulae in sheets that you have copied.

| Insert... |
| Delete |
| Rename |
| Move or Copy... |
| Select All Sheets |
| View Code |

Move or Copy

Move selected sheets
To book:
Nested if statements.xls
Before sheet:
Sheet1
Sheet2
Sheet3
(move to end)
☐ Create a copy

OK
Cancel

How do I ...?

<u>Copy data from Excel to Word 97</u>

You can use the 'clipboard' to copy information from Excel to Word 97 or any of the other Microsoft Office 97 applications. **Click** on the taskbar to move from one application to the other. Or, you can **press 'Alt' 'Tab'** to move through the open applications. However, just using the 'Copy' and 'Paste' option creates an 'embedded' object in Word. This means that if you make changes to your source data (worksheet) these will not be automatically reflected in your word processing document.

To create a 'linked' object in Word so that it includes changes you have made in Excel, **select** the range of cells in Excel and **click** on **'Copy'**. **Move** into Word, and **place** the cursor where you want to insert the data and **click** on **'Edit', 'Paste Special'** to show this 'dialogue box'. **Click** on **'Paste link:'** and **'Microsoft Excel Worksheet Object'** and **'OK'**. You can now move and change the size of this object.

How do I ...?

<u>Use absolute cell references</u>

The 'absolute' key 'F4' (this is the function key F4 at the top of the keyboard) inserts dollar signs into cell references. You can use an 'absolute' cell reference to prevent changes while you are copying. This is useful if you are basing your formula on one cell, for example working out VAT, or a percentage discount.

When you enter the formula, **key-in** as usual but when the reference of the cell to be made 'absolute' appears on the 'formula bar', **press 'F4'**. Dollar signs are inserted into your cell reference. **Key-in** the rest of the formula, for example **=\$D\$4*17.5%**. If you want any other cell to be 'absolute', **press 'F4'** when you have placed its cell reference into the formula. Or, you can key-in the dollar signs from the keyboard.

Copy the formula in the usual way. However, remember that whatever row or column you copy it into, the cell reference \$D\$4 is always the same.

Without the dollar signs Excel will change the formula to make it relate to its new row or column (see page 68).

How do I ...?

Use mixed cell references

You can make cells 'absolute' (see page 100). However, you may need to make part of a cell reference 'absolute' and leave the rest as 'relative' (see page 68). This is called a mixed cell reference.

Key-in the dollar sign in front of either the column or the row reference, for example $A3. When you copy this the 'A' stays the same but the row reference will change from 3 to 4 to 5, and so on. Or, A$3 would allow the 'A' to change to 'B' and 'C' but the row reference would stay at '3'.

How do I ...?

<u>Make one cell equal to another</u>

When you design your spreadsheet you need to think carefully about how you will use it. If, for example, you are doing a household budget, it may be that you are making the same payment each month. If you enter each payment separately, you will have to make any change to each cell individually or copy them.

However, if you link the cells together, change one payment and it will change all the ones that follow it, but not the ones that come before it.

	Rent			Rent
Jan	300		**Jan**	300
Feb	300		**Feb**	=B2
Mar	300		**Mar**	=B3
Apr	300		**Apr**	=B4
May	300		**May**	=B5
Jun	300		**Jun**	=B6
Jul	300		**Jul**	=B7

In this example, **'300'** was **keyed-in** to cell **B2**. In cell B3 the formula **=B2** was entered. **Key-in** = and then **click** on cell **B2** and 'Enter'. This was copied down into the rest of the column as shown opposite. Each cell is then 'equal to' the one before.

How do I ...?

Make one cell equal to others

Once you have set the formula up to make cells equal, it is a simple matter to make changes.

In the example given on page 102, if your rent was increased in May, you would only have to change the May figure and the others would automatically change, as shown below.

	Rent
Jan	300
Feb	300
Mar	300
Apr	300
May	350
Jun	350
Jul	350

Always plan your spreadsheet carefully so that it will work for you. Spend time on the design stage to make it as effective as you can.

How do I ...?

<u>Link cells</u>

You may want to link a cell through from one worksheet to another or from different workbooks. The 'target' cell is where you will enter the formula and the calculation displayed and the 'source' cell is the data you will use.

To link worksheets, **click** on the 'target' cell, and **key-in =**. Move back to the 'source' worksheet, and **click** on the original cell and **'Enter'** the formula. This will show on the 'formula bar' of the 'target' worksheet as **'=Sheet1!C2'** where the worksheet is 'Sheet 1' and the linked cell is 'C2'.

To link between workbooks, 'Open' both workbooks. **Click** on the 'target' cell and **key-in =**. **Press 'Ctrl Tab'** key or **click** on 'Window' menu and **click** on the name of the other workbook, in this example 'Books.xls'. **Click** on the 'source' cell and **'Enter'** the formula. This will show on the 'formula bar' of the 'target' worksheet as **= '[Books.xls]Sheet1'!$C$2**. This is now an 'absolute' reference (see page 100). Excel uses the 'exclamation mark' (!) to separate the sheets from the cells.

How do I ...?

<u>Create formulae using cells from different worksheets or different workbooks</u>

You can create formulae which use the information in cells from different worksheets or workbooks. To add together cells from different worksheets, the easiest way is to **click** on the cells you need.

For example, if you want to insert a formula on 'Sheet 1' which adds 'C10' from 'Sheet 1' and 'A3' from 'Sheet 2' and 'F4' from 'Sheet 3', you could key-in the formula. However, it is easy to make mistakes, so use the 'click method'.

Position the 'active cell' on 'Sheet 1' where you want to insert the formula and **key-in =**. **Click** on 'C10' on 'Sheet 1'. and the cell reference is inserted on the 'formula bar'. **Key-in +**. **Click** on 'Sheet 2' and **click** on cell 'A3'. This is now added to the formula. **Key-in +**. **Click** on 'Sheet 3' and **click** on cell 'F4'. **'Enter'** the formula. It should now read:

=C10+Sheet2!A3+Sheet3!F4. (There is no sheet reference for 'C10' because it is on the same sheet as the cell where you are going to insert the formula.) Use the same method to enter formulae across workbooks, but move between the workbooks with 'Window' or 'Ctrl' 'Tab'.

How do I ...?

Use functions across a range of worksheets

If you want to use a function using the same cells in different worksheets and these worksheets are next to each other, you can create a 'three-dimensional reference'. If you want to add together all the cells with the reference 'C10' over worksheets 1, 2 and 3, the formula would be **=SUM('Sheet1:Sheet3'!C10)**.

Again, it is easier to use the 'click method' rather than key-in the formula. This time you will have to use the 'Shift' key.

Move the 'active cell' where you want to insert the formula. **Key-in =sum(** and **click** on cell 'C10'. **Hold down** the 'Shift' key and **click** on 'Sheet 3'. The 'formula bar' will now display the formula given above. Note that Excel uses the 'colon' to show the range of sheets from 'Sheet 1' to 'Sheet 3'. An 'exclamation mark' separates the sheets from the cells.

How do I ...?

<u>Use templates</u>

You can use 'templates' for different styles, layouts and settings for your documents. Some 'templates' are already loaded in 'Excel'. To choose one of these, **click** on **'File'**, **'New'** to display this 'dialogue box'. **Double click** on **'Invoice.xlt'** to load the invoice template.

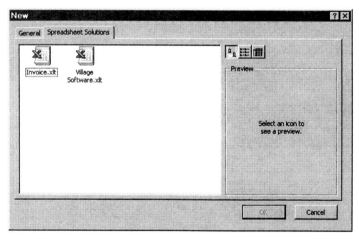

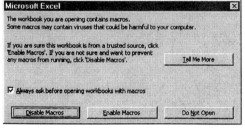

You will see this warning, read it carefully. **Click** on 'Enable Macros'. You can now use this format for your own invoices. You can find other 'templates' on the Internet.

How do I ...?

<u>Create and save my own template</u>

You can create your own 'templates' by setting up a new 'workbook' exactly as you want it. (See pages 60, 61, 62, 63, 84, 85 for formatting text and colours).

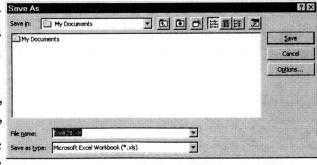

To save as a 'template' **click** on 'Save' button to display the 'Save As' dialogue box. **Key-in** your filename and **click** on ▼ next to 'Save as type box:' **Click** on **'Template (*.xlt)**. The file will be saved as a template with **.xlt** as its file extension. The screen changes to show 'Templates' in the 'Save in:' box replacing 'My Documents'.

To make this template appear in the 'New' 'dialogue box', you must save it in the correct folder. **Double click** on **'Spreadsheet Solutions'** and save. **Click** on **'File', 'New', Spreadsheet Solutions'** to show your own template.

How do I ...?

<u>Create a check box in a template</u>

You can create different boxes within your template to make it easier to use. **Show** the 'Forms' 'toolbar' (see page 19). **Click** on the 'Check Box'  button and the mouse pointer changes to +. **Click** and **drag** a rectangle at the point where you want this box to appear.

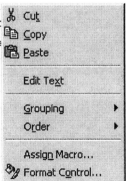

Point at the box frame and **click** the right mouse button for the 'shortcut menu'. **Click** on **'Edit Text'** to change the label for the button. 'Format Control' allows you to fill the box with colour, put a line around it, change its size and add 3-D shading to the tick box, amongst other things.

When you point to this box, a small flat hand with a pointing finger appears. **Click** and the box is 'checked', in other words it contains a tick. **Click** again to remove the tick and the box is 'unchecked'.

How do I ...?

Create a drop-down list in a template

Click on the 'Combo Box' button on the 'Forms' 'toolbar'. **Click** and **drag** to make a rectangle at the point where you need the box. A box is drawn with a down arrow shown inside it. It is selected, in other words it has small square boxes called 'handles' around it. **Click** on the box with the right mouse button to show the 'shortcut menu' and **click** on **'Format Control'**.

When the cursor is flashing in 'Input Range' **drag** it over the cells which contain the items for the drop-down list or use 'Collapse' button. You can also choose the number of lines in the box. If this is less than the number you need, a 'scroll bar' will automatically appear in the drop-down box.

When using the box, **click** on the down arrow and the list is displayed. **Click** on the item you need and it will be placed in the box. If you do not want to see the cells which contain the items for the list, you can 'hide' these (see page 123).

How do I ...?

Use a spreadsheet for 'What If' predictions

Spreadsheets are very useful in financial forecasting. It may be a simple budget that you are using, but you can see what effect any changes in income and spending would have. This is called a 'What If' prediction.

In this cashflow forecast, the cells that contain the important information, like the cost of goods and selling price are separate to the rest of the data. All the calculations are then based upon those cells. To see what would happen if the cost of coffee increased, all you need to do is to change one cell and the whole spreadsheet will change. See 'absolute references' on page 100.

CASHFLOW FORECAST FOR COFFEE

COST OF CUP OF COFFEE	£0.070	SELLING PRICE PER CUP OF COFFEE	£0.80

MONTH	CUPS OF COFFEE SOLD	PROFIT PER CUP	PROFIT FOR MONTH
January	100	£0.73	£73.00
February	150	£0.73	£109.50
March	200	=$D$2-$B$2	=C8*B8
April	250	=$D$2-$B$2	=C9*B9
May	300	=$D$2-$B$2	=C10*B10
June	350	£0.73	£255.50

How do I ...?

Use 'IF' statements

You can make your spreadsheet carry out a calculation only if certain conditions are true and to do something different if the conditions are false. In this spreadsheet the word 'REORDER' will appear when the stock of paper drops below 100 reams.

	A	B	C	D	E	F
1		STOCK RECORD OF BOOKS				
2						
3	DATE	ITEM	NO IN	NO OUT	BALANCE	REORDER
4	04/01/99	REAMS OF COPIER PAPER	500		500	
5	04/01/99	REAMS OF COPIER PAPER		150	350	
6	05/01/99	REAMS OF COPIER PAPER		200	150	
7	07/01/99	REAMS OF COPIER PAPER		60	90	REORDER
8	09/01/99	REAMS OF COPIER PAPER		10	80	REORDER

In column 'F' you will insert the following formula in cell 'F4' and copy it into the rest of the column **=IF(E4<100,"REORDER","")**. The spreadsheet reads the number in cell 'E4' and if it is less than (<) (see page 26) 100, 'REORDER' appears in cell 'F4'. If the number is more than 100, the cell is left blank . The 'IF' statement is enclosed in brackets and commas separate the steps of the calculation. Double quotes enclose the text you are going to insert and 2 double quotes together mean that nothing is input.

How do I ...?

Use Paste Function to create IF statements

Click on the cell where you are going to insert the formula. **Click** on the Paste Function button to display this 'dialogue box'. **Click** on 'Logical' in the 'Function category' box and **click** on 'IF' in the 'Function name' box and 'OK'.

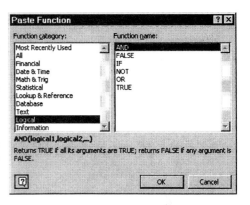

This second 'dialogue box' appears. **Click** in 'Logical_test' and **key-in** the first condition. For the example in page 112 this would be 'E4<100'.

In the next box 'Value_if_true' **key-in** REORDER. In the 'Value_if_false' box, **key-in** "". This shows there is nothing to put in there if the argument is false. **Click** on 'OK' and the formula is created for you.

How do I ...?

Use more than one 'IF' statement

Using an 'IF' statement allows you to make calculations based on whether certain information is true or false. However, you can only have 2 calculations in one 'IF' statement. You can join the 'IF' statements together up to 7 to increase the number of criteria you can choose.

=IF(G2<$C$2,"ORDER "&$B$2-G2,IF(G2>$C$2,G2-$C$2))

What this means is that if G2 is less than C2, put ORDER and the product of B2 – G2 in H2. If G2 is more than C2, put the product of G2 – C2 in H2.

	A	B	C	D	E	F	G	H
1	DATE	MAX	MIN	CURRENT	IN	OUT	ACTUAL	REORDER/ No above min le
2		1000	500	600		200	400	ORDER 600
3				400	600	50	950	
4				950		300	650	
5				650		300	350	ORDER 650

There is always an opening bracket after 'IF'. A comma separates each different step and the number of brackets at the end of the formula is equal to the number of 'IF's in the statement. This is called 'nesting' IF statements.

How do I ...?

Name a cell or range of cells

You can give individual cells or a range of cells a name which you then use instead of the cell reference. You can use this name to quickly move to that range of cells in your worksheet, for printing out the range of cells, in formulae and also 'lookup tables' (see page 118). Remember if you are using a named range as a 'lookup table', you must sort the first column in ascending order.

Select the cell or range of cells you want to name. **Click** at the left of the 'formula bar' in the [Bonus ▼] 'Name Box' and **key-in** the name. Or, **click** on **'Insert', 'Name', 'Define'** and **key-in** the name. This must begin with a letter or an underscore character (_), it must not contain any spaces and you can use up to 255 characters.

To move to the named range, **click** on ▼ at the side of the 'Name Box' and **click** on the name in the 'drop-down' box. The range of cells is then highlighted. To remove a name, **click** on **'Insert', 'Name' 'Define'**, **click** on the name and **click** on **'Delete'**.

How do I ...?

<u>Sort data</u>

To sort into order, **move** the 'active cell' in the column you want to sort and **click** on the 'Sort Ascending' $\frac{A}{Z}\downarrow$ button or the 'Sort Descending' $\frac{Z}{A}\downarrow$ button. This will sort data into alphabetical or numerical order. You should key-in names with the surname first if you are sorting into alphabetical order.

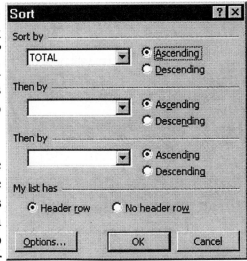

If the same data is contained in more than one cell in a column, you can sort on more than one column. **Click** on **'Data', 'Sort'** to display this 'dialogue box'. The heading of the first column is shown in the 'Sort by' box. **Click** on ▼ to change it. **Click** on **'Ascending'** or **'Descending'** and **click** in the 'Then by' box to choose a second and third column as needed. **Click** on **'OK'**.

How do I ...?

Use the filter

If you need to take information from your spreadsheet, you can use the AutoFilter facility. A filtered list shows only rows that contain data you choose.

Click on a cell inside the column which contains the data you want to choose.

3	NAME ▾	J∤▾	F∤▾	M∤▾	A∤▾
7	R Ardron	1200	1150	1400	1500
8	C Vaughan	1350	900	1400	1750
9	S Rowley	750	1000	1200	1165

Click on **'Data'**, **'Filter'**, **'AutoFilter'** and arrows appear at the top of the columns. **Click** on the arrow at the top of the column containing data you want to use. **Select '(Custom)'** to make your own choices, or **'(Top 10 ...)'** to list the top or bottom 10 items. **Select 'Percent'** under **'Items'** to find the top or bottom value in your list. Or, **click** on one of the numbers to find only items that match that number. **Click** on **'(All)'** to show all the data and **'Data'**, **'Filter'**, **'Autofilter'** to remove the filter.

(All)
(Top 10...)
(Custom...)
1165
1265
1450
1475
1500
1750
(Blanks)
(NonBlanks)

How do I ...?

Define a LOOKUP formula

The 'LOOKUP' function looks in a table (a named range of cells), finds the information you need and puts the data from the table into your 'active cell'. An example of a VLOOKUP formula in cell 'J4' is =VLOOKUP(H4,Bonus,2). This contains 3 separate pieces of information (arguments) as shown below.

	H	I	J
1			
2			
3	TOTAL	COMM	BONUS
4	9765	£1,953	80
5	10395	£2,079	100
6	8432	£1,686	80
7	8585	£1,717	80
8	8900	£1,780	80
9	7281	£1,456	60
10	5555	£1,111	0

What? - the value to check for in the 'lookup table' **(H4)**.

Where? - the name of the 'lookup table' – Excel automatically looks in column one of that table **(Bonus)**. ◄──────►

Which? - the column number in the 'lookup table' from which the data is taken and placed in the 'active cell' **(2)**.

TOTAL	BONUS
5000	0
6000	60
8000	80
10000	100

This means that the total in 'H4' is compared with the figures in column one of the Bonus Table. The amount of Bonus earned is selected from column 2 and returned to cell 'J4' the 'active cell'. VLOOKUP shows the data is compared vertically in columns, HLOOKUP compares data horizontally.

How do I ...?

Create a 'VLOOKUP' function

Click in the cell where you want to insert the formula. **Click** on the 'Paste Function' button and under 'Function Category' **click** on **'Lookup & reference'**. In the 'Function Name' box, **click** on **'VLOOKUP'**. **Click** on **'OK'**. This 'dialogue box' is displayed. The first column of the 'lookup table' must be in ascending order.

VLOOKUP		
Lookup_value		= any
Table_array		= number
Col_index_num		= number
Range_lookup		= logical

=
Searches for a value in the leftmost column of a table, and then returns a value in the same row from a column you specify. By default, the table must be sorted in an ascending order.
Lookup_value is the value to be found in the first column of the table, and can be a value, a reference, or a text string.

Formula result =   OK   Cancel

In 'Lookup_value' box, **key-in** or **drag** over the cell reference of the cell whose value you are checking against the table. **Press 'Tab'** key to move to 'Table_array' box. **Key-in** the name of your table. In 'Col_index_num' box **key-in** the column of the table whose value you will enter in the 'active cell'. 'Range_lookup' is an optional entry. **Key-in 'true'** (or leave blank) to find the nearest match and **'false'** for an exact match.

How do I ...?

<u>Change a 'lookup table'</u>

Once you have created your 'VLOOKUP' function (see pages 118 and 119), you can add or remove information from your 'lookup table'. Or, you can edit the data and the changes will be made automatically to your spreadsheet without you having to change your formula.

Experiment with using the different 'Lookup tables'. Create an 'HLOOKUP' table horizontally in rows and a 'VLOOKUP' table vertically in columns.

How do I ...?

Freeze panes

When your worksheet is very large, you may want to see the column headings as you scroll through your spreadsheet. You can do this with 'Freeze Panes'.

Select the row below where you want to make a split. **Click** on **'Window'**, **'Freeze Panes'**. As you move through your worksheet, the frozen rows stay at the top of the screen and the rows below move. To remove the setting, **click** on **'Windows' 'Unfreeze Panes'**.

You can also freeze the columns at the left edge of the spreadsheet. **Select** the column to the right of where you want to make the split. **Click** on **'Windows'**, **'Freeze Panes'**.

How do I ...?

Split the screen

You can split your screen using the 'Split' box at the top of the vertical scroll bar.

Drag the 'Split' box onto the spreadsheet where you want to make the split. To remove the split, **double click** on the split.

Or, you can use 'Window', 'Split' to turn a split on and off.

You can use **'F6'** to move to the different panes.

How do I ...?

<u>Hide and Unhide columns and rows</u>

You can hide parts of your spreadsheet from view, either:

- for confidentiality reasons;
- to make a large sheet more manageable and see only the data you need; or
- to leave out portions from the printout.

Select the row or columns you want to hide and **click** the right mouse button for the 'shortcut menu' and **click** on **'Hide'**. Or, **'Format'**, **'Row'**, **'Hide'** to hide a row, **'Format'**, **'Column'**, **'Hide'** to hide a column or **'Window'**, **'Hide'** for the current workbook. The row above the 'active cell' is hidden or the column to the right of the 'active cell'. A line appears in the spreadsheet to show where cells are missing and the row numbers and column letters stay the same. Any formulae which include the hidden cells will not be changed.

✂ Cut
▤ Copy
▤ Paste
Paste Special...
Insert
Delete
Clear Contents
▦ Format Cells...
Row Height...
Hide
Unhide

To get the cells back, **select** the row above and below the line, or the column to the left and right of the line and **click** on **'Unhide'** from the 'shortcut menu'.

How do I ...?

<u>Work with Pivot tables</u>

You can summarise, analyse, organise and compare large amounts of information in your worksheet using a 'pivot table'. This type of table is named 'pivot' because you can change the column and row headings around to give different tables. In other words you can 'pivot' the table. You can use data from a spreadsheet or database such as 'Microsoft Access', 'ORACLE', 'FoxPro' and so on.

In this example of a 'pivot table', you would click on to drop down a list of car models. You could then choose a model and the data would be summarised for you to compare the sales of different areas in the region.

MODEL	(All)				
Sum of WEEKLY SALES	MAKE				
YORKSHIRE REGION	Ford	Rover	Vauxhall	Volkswagon	Grand Total
Bradford			30	11	41
Huddersfield	9	1	5		15
Leeds		3	22		25
Sheffield		3	21		24
Wakefield	7	2	12		21
Grand Total	16	9	90	11	126

MODEL	Corsa	
Sum of WEEKLY SALES	MAKE	
YORKSHIRE REGION	Vauxhall	Grand Total
Huddersfield	5	5
Leeds	22	22
Grand Total	27	27

Information Technology Resources – User Guide for Excel 97
© ITR 1999

How do I ...?

Create a pivot table 1

Open the spreadsheet on which you will create the 'pivot table'. **Move** the 'active cell' to the beginning of the data you want to summarise. **Click** on **'Data', 'Pivot Table Report'** to show this 'dialogue box'. You can choose where your data is coming from, this will be 'Microsoft Excel list or database' unless you change it. **Click** on **'Next'** to show this second page of the 'PivotTable Wizard'.

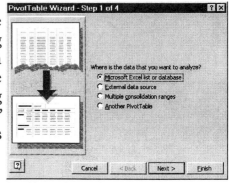

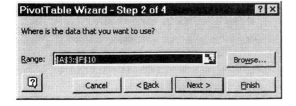

Excel automatically chooses a range of cells around the 'active cell'. If this is correct, **click** on **'Next'**, if not, **drag** across the correct cells.

How do I ...?

Create a pivot table 2

Choose the layout of your 'pivot table'. The column headings for your spreadsheet are listed on the right. **Drag** these across and place them in 'ROW' if they are to be row headings and 'COLUMN' if they are to be column headings. **Drag** the heading for the column containing the data you want to analyse into the 'DATA' area. This will summarise the values in the table. 'PAGE' allows you to show data for one item at a time in the table. **Drag** a

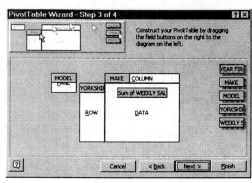

heading into 'PAGE'. **Click** on 'Next'.

At this fourth page of the 'PivotTable Wizard' you can choose to put the 'pivot table' into a new worksheet or within your existing worksheet. **Click** on the cell where the table is to begin. **Click** on 'Finish'.

How do I ...?

Add and remove fields from a pivot table

Move the 'active cell' inside the 'pivot table'. On the 'pivot table toolbar', **click** on the 'Pivot Table Wizard' 🖽 button. This will display the 'Step 3 of 4' 'dialogue box' for the Wizard (see page 126).

Once again, all your column headings are listed on the right of the box. **Drag** the other heading into the area where you need it. **Click** on **'Finish'**. Using this method, you can add extra items to your table.

To delete a 'field', **select** the field (this cell will be shaded) in your 'pivot table' and **drag** it outside the area of the table. The mouse pointer becomes a button with a large cross over it. Release the mouse button and the field is deleted. Remember to use 'Undo' if you make a mistake.

Once created you can easily update a 'pivot table' and use it to create charts. Any changes made to data in the Excel spreadsheet on which the 'pivot table' is based, will not show until you update the 'pivot table' using the 'Refresh Data' ! button.